Real Men Get Breast Cancer

So what's the big deal about getting breast cancer?

Frank F. Harmon III

Frank & Sandy Harmon

"A special thanks to my wife Sandy for being there for me every step of the way."

ISBN: 978-1-300-14315--4

Table of Contents

Forward

So what's the big deal about breast cancer, you get it, you have some surgery, you take some chemo, maybe some radiation and that's that; you go on with your life…hopefully. Breast cancer is responsible for taking the lives of approximately 41,000 women in the United States every year. Approximately 270,000 women will be diagnosed with breast cancer in this country every year. It is second only to heart disease in altering and destroying lives. Approximately 1/10th of 1% of the breast cancer cases diagnosed in a year are men. That is why there is so little press about it.

I opened with a rather cavalier statement hoping to annoy someone into reading further to see what this pompous individual had to say about the subject. I'm no doctor, I'm no expert, I am a male who has survived breast cancer and my purpose here is to support the women who endure this experience and educate men about the potential of their own breast cancer. I also hope to offer guidance and observation from my very personal experience, as to what those undergoing treatment, are dealing with. Men and women view most things differently and the following are my male views of a historically female issue.

Anything written in here that sounds medical or "doctorish" came from a report because I have no such training. I am a Commercial General Building

Contractor so I think in terms of concrete, steel and block. I deal with schedules, inspectors and pay apps so emotion, pain and fear have not been part of my life…until now.

I dedicate this to the memory of my mother Alice who died in 1966 from this disease, to her sister Lucille who died in 1963 from this disease, to my sister Cathy who survived this disease in 1988, to my stepmother Helene who survived this disease in 1991 and to my niece Ashlie who survived this disease with me in 2009. Breast cancer, through the years, has run rampant through my family affecting at least three generations that we know of. Hopefully it stops here with me.

I give thanks to all who helped me through this, God, my family, my friends the doctors and most importantly, my wife, Sandy.

To obtain more copies of this book or to download the song, "The Gift of Love" contained within, please visit www.SongsForCause.org.

The History

In the beginning, God created heaven and earth and other good things for us to enjoy; perhaps he also created cancer to keep us in check.

In my beginning, my mother and her sister died from breast cancer driven problems way back in the mid 60s. I always thought that 44 years old was much too early to leave this earth, but what did I know, I was only 19. The years have gone by and I have three daughters of my own and, being a responsible adult, I have warned them of the breast cancer history in our family and told them about what my mother had to go through.

My younger sister had breast cancer at the young age of 36 and took the precautionary measures of having everything cancerous removed and reconstructed, as did my girls' Grandmother in her due time. The topic of this disease was never far from discussion and awareness of it has always been keen.

My sister found out about a BRCA 1 and BRCA 2 genetic test, by which you could determine if you were a likely breast cancer genetic carrier, or had cellular deficiencies in that area or something like that.

With our family history, she having one daughter and I having three, it seemed to be a good idea for us to get the test done. As it turns out; she was positive and I was negative. Being negative was a good thing because now, my daughters were at no greater risk of breast cancer than any other woman. We really thought very little about it until November 4, 2008, when I found out that I had breast cancer.

"WHAT !! YOU MUST BE FREAKING KIDDING ME !! THAT'S IMPOSSIBLE, I'M A MALE, I DON'T EVEN HAVE BREASTS!! I RIDE A HARLEY AND DO MANLY THINGS, YOUR FREAKING TESTS ARE ALL WRONG !!"
I started to cry (it was ok because I was by myself)

I was taking a shower one day and while washing my chest, I felt a funny sensation under my left nipple. It wasn't painful, but it alerted me enough to check it further. I felt around with my fingers and detected a mass directly under the nipple and as I squeezed it, it hurt. This freaked me out because the thoughts, "breast lump", "cancer" and "my mother dying" immediately came to mind and it did not feel comforting. I asked my wife what she thought it was (I figured that she would know being a woman and also having worked in a hospital operating room for 34 years). Her answer was "we better have a doctor look at it soon".

As luck would have it, Sandy was scheduled for a routine colonoscopy on the next Thursday and her surgeon's partner had agreed to examine me that day in the Doctor's lounge (I was the designated driver). After feeling the lump, he scheduled me for an immediate mammogram, an ultrasound and an ultrasound guided biopsy (if needed). It was kinda neat because he walked me to the sign in desk and said "this man is a friend of mine, he has breast cancer and I want these tests performed immediately." I liked the friend of mine bit but not the breast cancer statement.

Soooooo, off I go to the "Women's Hospital".

The Diagnosis

Ok, so I agree that a "woman's hospital" is not a good place for a man to be a patient. I was taken into a room with about twenty women sitting there all dressed in paper sheets. They were looking at me like I was an arsonist holding a lighted match and gave me the feeling that, clearly, I had no business entering their "inner sanctuary". I could not agree more with them but, I was just following orders.

I was led down a hallway to a room, told to take my shirt off and step up to the machine. The technician said, "Lean in and put your breast on the plate." "You must be kidding", I said, "I don't have a breast." "Yes you do", said Nurse Ratchet, "just push harder against the edge of the plate." I did and then, it was as if she dropped a guillotine on my skin because suddenly, there emerged a "breast" pinched between the two plates.

> ***Guy note:*** *This feels like getting your finger slammed in the car door.*

There it was, a "2.4 x 2.1 cm hypermetabolic mass with irregular borders".

The ultrasound table was cold and hard but the technician was not. Actually she was quite skilled with the equipment and quickly found the mass under the nipple. Her experience told her to look further so she tracked down my left side and found lymph nodes that were also enlarged. It was determined that biopsies should be taken of the mass under the nipple and also of the lymph nodes in the axilla area.

> ***Guy note:*** *Axilla is what doctors call the armpit.*

So far, this has not been a "physically unpleasant" procedure but, that was about to change. With an ultrasound-guided biopsy, the location of the mass is identified using the ultrasound paddle, which shows the location of the "gigantic pencil sized NEEDLE" that they have just inserted into to you, relative to the location of the mass. You then hear (and feel) a loud click, and a portion of the mass is retracted by the needle apparatus. They put the sample into a jar for lab analysis; then move on to the axilla.

> ***Guy note:*** *The click sounds like a staple gun and is innocent enough however, the feeling part is like stapling something to the end of your nose.*

Author's note, I haven't actually done this but can imagine what it would feel like.

I finished with my tests and got back to where my wife was as she was coming out of the anesthesia. The tests showed that she was just fine but we would soon learn that my journey was just about to begin.

Newly found emotion: This is scary. No missed field-goal or dropped pass can compare to the utter despair surging through your mind when you do not know the results of the tests and have to spend the entire weekend worrying about it. No amount of someone saying, "it will be ok", or other positive thinking will help. You are sure that it is bad and are just as sure that you are going to die.

You become emotionally exhausted and a serious dark cloud hangs over your being as you start thinking of all the things that you need to do before you die. This is when you make your "bucket list", because it's the "C" word and cancer is never good.

> **Guy note:** *If your spouse is going through this, all you can do is be there. She doesn't want to be held or coddled. Well, yes she does but not right now. Well when then? I don't know. Nothing you can say will be right. Well it could be but I don't know when. She is completely engulfed in her own feeling of despair and gloom and won't know what she wants until she finds out that she wants it.*
>
> *By then, it will probably be too late and you should have known anyway. It's a time of emotional meltdown and all you can do is be there when she needs you. As guys, we don't understand this "not knowing" stuff but women do. Sandy was there for me without my asking. All you can do is stay close.*

Well, the weekend finally ended and while I was at work Monday, I got the call from the pathologist. I was the proud owner of a 2.5 cm invasive ductal carcinoma, stage 3, T2, estrogen and progesterone positive whatever, whatever, whatever. I stopped listening and pulled over to the side of the road and called Sandy. I knew it, now I'm going to die, but we scheduled the surgery for the upcoming Thursday anyway.

The Surgery

It was immediately decided that surgery was the first necessary procedure and although there was no cancer detected on my right side, I was not going to take the chance of leaving something behind to be a possible second round of it, so…bilateral mastectomy, scheduled for Thursday.

Now, I never even really pondered the fact that men have breasts. I have certainly pondered women's breasts but not my own. I mean, we don't have any – at least not any that are worth mentioning. Evidently, we do have breast tissue, nipples, duct work and such. Even considering the fact that breast cancer had been such a decimator of my family, I never considered that it could happen to me. Men get prostate cancer not breast cancer, how absurd.

Doctor "E" was scheduled to do my surgery. Some call him Dr. E because they can't pronounce his last name. The day of the surgery, a few friends and family were in the pre-surgery room with

Sandy and me, laughing and cutting up, trying to keep my spirits up. I did not have any real misgivings about the surgery itself because I was confident of the skill of the people caring for me.

Sandy has worked in this Operating Room for over three decades and as a result of her friendship with the doctors and nurses, the best-of-the-best signed on to be on my case. I had nothing to worry about from a surgical point of view, but was in turmoil regarding the cancer in general, along with its causes and effects, and with my future on this planet. One of my daughters referred to Dr. E as Doctor McDreamy and felt that he was the best part of my hospital adventure.

I was rolled back into the cold, stark room. With my blue-speckled gown and IV hooked in, I was ready to go. My blood pressure was normal, 116/80 with a pulse of 66 (this is pretty normal for me) and when they asked if I wanted something to calm me down, I asked, "does it look like I need it?". They gave it to me anyway….off to lala land.

During the surgery, of which I remember nothing, I was cut from axilla to axilla. Any and all mammary tissue, nipples and duct work were removed. A dye which lit up the lymph system was injected, giving Dr. E a "roadmap" to follow so he could remove any cancer-infected lymph nodes. As cancer cells move from the original site (in my case the left nipple) to other places about the body, they necessarily must pass through the lymph nodes.

I learned that lymph nodes are like a basket strainer in the kitchen sink, they catch the crap that shouldn't go down the drain, in this case, cancer cells. Lymph nodes are tiny bean shaped organs through which lymph vessels flow. Lymph in general, is a fluid contained within a system of vessels that help to fight infection and disease and this lymph moves throughout your body. Sentinel nodes are the first ones in line – Dr. E removed five on the right side. The pathology group said that they were free of cancer so the right side was done.

The left side was a different matter. We already knew that cancer had spread to the lymph system on that side so the surgery was destined to be much more extensive – and it sure was. Twenty-one nodes were removed before the pathology report came back negative. Thirteen of the twenty-one removed had cancer in them. At this time I was supposedly cancer free by the hands of Dr. E. He was confident that all the cancerous tissue, nodes and other bad stuff that he could find had been removed. Well, this is a good thing isn't it?

> ***Guy note:*** *Prior to this surgery, I had had an appendix removed, a hernia fixed and both knees scoped and repaired. I felt that I was a surgery-pro*

and this would be nothing in comparison. I couldn't have been more wrong.

"OH MY GOD!!!!!!!!! What happened! I came in here for a mastectomy so why does everything ELSE hurt?...You did what? A foley catheter? What's that?" (A garden hose wrapped with sandpaper?) The first thing that I remembered while waking up was someone removing the foley. It really did feel like someone was pulling a 20 foot long piece of rusty re-bar out of my body.

My chest was on fire and it felt like someone had gone from armpit to armpit with a router (which is a woodworking tool – not part of the internet). I could not believe how much everything hurt. Finally, Ms. "nurse from heaven" injected some morphine into my IV and everything began to get better, much better.

Eventually, I said goodbye to everybody in post-op and they took Sandy and me off to my "hotel suite" for the night. The room had a nice bed, which folds in the middle, it is not very comfortable and it's like sleeping on a sawhorse. I was cut from armpit-to-armpit, (I mean axilla-to-axilla), double and triple taped across my chest, and had what felt like garden hoses sutured into my sides. The "garden hoses" were hooked up to a couple of suction bulbs (like a turkey baster) and they were drawing a pinkish fluid from my axillas. So there I was, lying on my back, hooked up to what seemed like every wire and tube they had in the hospital and of course, realized that I had to use the restroom.

The nurse promptly handed me a plastic bottle. As it turned out, no part of me was willing or able to do this rolling over to hit the bottle thing, especially with an audience. Instead, Sandy helped me across the room to the bathroom with my entire "internet" of tubes and wires with me.

I realized then that my sense of control over my body was gone and that the road ahead wouldn't be as black-and-white as I had expected. Big Ed finally cooperated and I emptied my bladder. For now though, I discovered peace in the morphine drip, and went to sleep. Sandy went home to get some rest herself.

Healing at Home

The healing process begins and ends at home. Everything hurts, even areas that were not directly affected by the surgery. You compensate for the pain in the surgical area by using some other part of your body that is not designed for that purpose. Then it starts to hurt because it is not used to the activity that you are assigning to it. I have a very difficult time sleeping on my back. I can't, but you have to when your front is so torn up.

Therefore, sleep does not come in one nice restful group, it comes in a multitude of naps and short periods of "nodding off", that are rudely interrupted by pain or another bathroom trip. They say, "remember to rest and drink plenty of liquids." What's that all about anyway… drinking plenty of liquids leads to plenty of bathroom trips…which means getting out of bed and with that, more pain. It is hard to comply with that great advice!

My mastectomy was done with no consideration for reconstruction. I mean, why bother, I don't need breasts for anything. I remember before the surgery, Dr. E drew a couple of ellipses on my chest. These were to be the cutting lines for the surgery – they looked like they could be the parts of a football if you were to disassemble one.

The resulting scars were two straight lines, each about eight to nine inches long. The skin was sewn together, then strapped tight and covered by enough tape to "tape up" the ankles of an entire defensive line. I guess Dr. E didn't want me to come apart.

One of the more annoying aspects of the healing was the cavity drains. A piece of tubing was inserted into the bottom of the voids in my axillas, which had been created by the removal of tissue (lymph nodes et al). This tubing was sutured to my skin, leaving residual stabbing pains when I moved.

The outside end of this tubing was hooked to a bulb that was depressed creating a negative pressure. As the bulb inflated itself, it withdrew fluids from the cavity and these fluids had to be measured and emptied on a regular basis. I am not sure what the fluids were, where they came from or why they were there, but Dr. E said that they were to be expected and to just deal with it.

"Dealing with it" became a bit of trouble because initially the bulbs were pinned to the mound of tape holding my chest together. As the tape came off, so came off the place to pin the bulbs and I found myself pinning them to the inside of a T-shirt. That system worked fairly well as long as I remembered to un-hook the bulbs before I took off the T-shirt. I forgot to do this only one time.

Showering was also a fun experience because without the T shirt, there was no place to pin the bulbs so I bent a clothes hanger in such a fashion that it would go around my neck and hung the bulbs from that contraption. I was going to patent this idea but now, I give it freely to you.

> ***Guy note:*** *Ok, you have had surgeries like hernia, knee, appendix and stuff like that right? Guess what, put them all together and you haven't begun to touch this one. This is major ouchness. It hurts and it is real. If your wife tells you " I'm ok, just go and relax and I'll be ok", it is BS, do not listen to her because she is thinking about you and how this is affecting your situation.*
>
> *How you are affected is really irrelevant! She is in a great deal of pain and discomfort and needs pillow fluffing, blanket straightening a glass of water or whatever other thing you can think of. Just do it and just be there.*

Newly found emotion: I have just had parts of my body removed that have been with me forever. As a male, my breasts are of no use to me and over the years, I have barely noticed or even considered them being there. A woman however, in some ways, is identified as a woman by having them, so what must she be going through now? Is it like losing the "twins"? I can't imagine what is going through her mind. It must hurt as much as her body does.

You have no idea how much you use a certain part of your body until you can't use it any more. Simple things like holding a toothbrush, flossing, eating, holding a beer bottle, wiping, all involve your pecks at some level.

Think about it, there is no substitute muscle group you can re-train to do these things. You have no choice but to use the chest muscles – so you just get used to it.

Healing at the Doctor's Office

The whole "fluid-draining-into-the-bulbs" thing got old quickly. I was draining about 80 ml daily from the left side and 30 from the right. After approximately two weeks, the right side stopped draining and the left was down to 15 ml or less. It amazed me that the news Dr. E had to deliver would be such a "happy experience" – the drains could come out.

This was a glorious day for me because I had come to absolutely hate them being attached to me. It was quick and easy, into the office, shirt off, cut the sutures, pull out the tubes, tape up the holes and out the door I go. Free at last. Well…sort of.

The left side did not really stop draining as anticipated. Well it did, but not really. My body was still making fluids as it repaired itself, except that with the drains gone, there was no place for the fluid to go. "Well duh, it will just reabsorb." Not really, I became a human water balloon.

So, off to Dr E's I go with this sloshing bag under my armpit, I mean axilla, to see what he could do about it. He already knew what he was going to do but I just figured that he would simply "fix it". Well "simply" was a NEEDLE the diameter of a crayon that he inserted into the sloshing bag to let the fluid out.

This procedure was referred to as a "surgical aspiration" which is a professional way of saying "draining fluid out of a body pocket by sticking it with a really big needle". This activity repeated I think a total of eight times. I could go for three days or so before the buildup needed draining. It made the idea of "keeping the drains in a little longer", a good idea if I ever do this again.

> ***Guy note:*** *So, you have had your knee drained when fluid has built up on it because of some sports injury, but this is different. The armpit/axilla is a sensitive area, I mean really sensitive. Have some compassion here because it really does hurt when they put that needle in.*

Newly found emotion: All of the people with whom I have dealt, have been compassionate, caring people who go about their daily jobs with an air of professionalism and skill. Some have a sense of humor but I would imagine that good judgment would dictate that they should keep it in check when dealing with a patient. There is nothing that says that the patient can't be the clown.

These health care professionals at the hospitals and doctor's offices deal with sick, complaining, frightened, hurting people all day long and I decided that I would not be one of them. No matter how badly I felt, or how much I hurt, I tried to make them smile or laugh to make their day better. They were caring for me, why shouldn't I return the favor. I think that it worked because we both ended up happier.

Chemo Port Goes In

As I understand it, from a surgical point of view, I became cancer free the minute Dr. E sewed me up; however, that is not the end of the story. Cells in our bodies normally grow, divide and die in an orderly fashion.

Cancer cells divide faster than normal cells or do not die as they should and eventually can grow out of control and become a tumor.

When cancer cells spread from their original location, to other parts of the body via the blood or lymph system, it is then called metastatic cancer. If cancer travels from the breast and finds a home in the lungs or some place else, it is still called breast cancer. It is named for the place of its origin.

Round two of cancer treatment at least in my case, was to send out an army of cancer cell killers called chemotherapy drugs to track down any cells that may have escaped the lymph nodes. This is called adjuvant therapy and is given to target any cancer cells that cannot be detected and may have metastasized somewhere else.

The chemotherapy drugs, which I will get into later, are a pretty caustic mix of chemicals and need to be delivered intravenously.

Evidently, the strength of the drugs and the amount of time necessary to deliver them would compromise the integrity of the veins into which they would be administered so a device called a VAD (vascular access device) or port as most everybody calls it, was due to be installed by Dr.E.

The port is about ½ the diameter of a golf ball and if you were to slice off the top and bottom 25% of the golf ball, you have something about the size of the port. The port is made of titanium and has a rubber tube coming out of the bottom side edge of it. The hollowed out interior is filled with medical silicone.

The tube in inserted into your subclavian vein and then extended into the upper chamber of your heart where it terminates. When the procedure is complete, the end result is a suture line a couple of inches long and a bump under your skin. Mine was installed on my right side just below my collarbone.

The port allows access to your vascular system by providing an insertion point for a needle into the silicone.

Once the needle is withdrawn, the silicone repairs itself and the system is all sealed up again. This is an inventive contraption, but it hurts while being accessed. The port receives the chemotherapy drugs instead of your veins – remember the bit about caustic?

As the IV drips into the port, so drips the chemo into your heart where it is picked up and immediately diluted as it is whooshed throughout your body by your heartbeat. I had a real mental problem with this device being there.

Although I knew it was necessary for an overall good prognosis, I did not like it. It was hard to sleep on and my imagination allowed me to decide that it could possibly come apart and there I would be with a massive cardiac blowout as blood pumped back from my heart, up stream and out of this unattached tubing all over the ceiling, walls and bedding.

Sometimes I get the best of myself. Again, you get used to it.

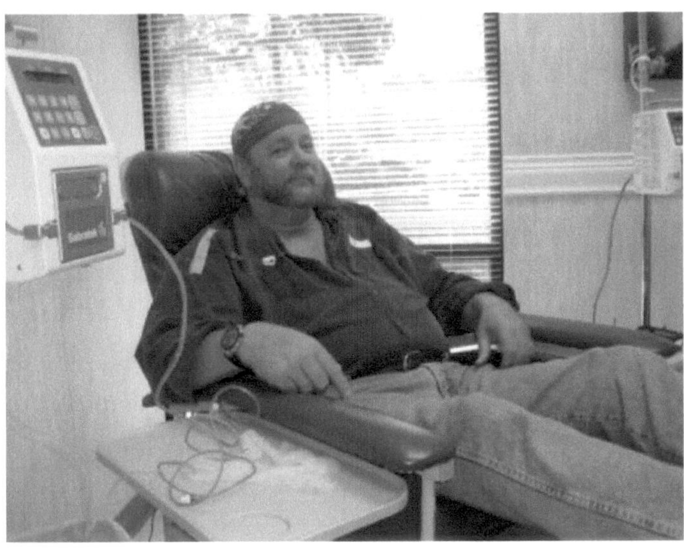

Frank in Chemotherapy

Chemo Treatment

I said I would explain more on chemo drugs "later" and it is now "later". Below is a portion of the statement that describes the drugs that were put into me. I make no claim as to knowing what any of this is other than it being a cocktail of drain-cleaner-type-stuff, measured specifically for my weight and designed to kill my cancer.

> ***Venipuncture:*** IV infusion, for therapy, prophylaxis, or diagnosis: addi seq nfusion, up to 1 hour.
>
> Therapeutic, prophylactic, or diagnostic injection, (specify substance or drug); each additional sequential intravenous push of a new substance/drug.
>
> - *Decadron 1MG*
> - *Aloxi 25 MCG*
> - *Adriamycin 10 MG*
> - *Cytoxin 100 MG*
> - *Cytoxin 200 MG*
> - *Cytoxin 1 G*

Ok, have to admit, this chemo thing really scared me. I can deal with surgery because I understand what is going to happen, they put me to sleep, cut, remove or repair something, sew me back up and wake me up. You deal with the pain and move on.

The chemo is a different deal because the treatment consists of four infusions three weeks apart of one drug and four infusions three weeks apart of another drug. I realized that I had absolutely no control of what was going to happen with chemo over the span of treatment, so I had to resign myself that I was simply along for the ride.

The chemo is designed to kill highly active cells. It cannot differentiate between cancerous and healthy cells so some good cells get killed. This also causes side effects that are not pleasant. Some side effects are as follows: nausea and vomiting, diarrhea, hair loss, fatigue, numbness and tingling in your hands or feet, nail changes, muscle pain, rash, stomatitis and changes in vision. There are multiple, spaced out infusions so that the greatest number of cancerous cells can be treated.

I admit that I was as scared as I have ever been in my life. The nurses however, are the absolute best on earth. They know that some of their patients will die, they know that some of their patients will get only marginally better and they know that all of their patients will get some degree of sick. They smile and they are gentle with their compassionate touch, they are wonderful people. My first nurse was Jean, she knew that I was scared out of my mind but "talked me off the ledge" and got things started.

So, how bad can this chemo thing really be? Let's find out. I'm sitting in the infusion chair, blood pressure 122/78, pulse rate 65, my heart faithfully pumping away, blissfully unaware that we are about to pump a couple of bags of toxins into it. My brain knows what is about to happen and has the rest of me scared. The nurse sees it and asks me if I want something to relax me; no thanks, let's just get started.

She takes a little bit of blood and goes away to the lab to analyze it leaving Sandy and me to sit there and wonder what's next. When she came back, it turned out that my blood had 3 to 5 times the minimum WBC, platelets required to administer chemo so, since it is "super blood", off we go to destroy it. The following is from a diary that I kept.

> ***Day 1*** *The infusion (Adriamycin/Cytoxin) takes six hours and is painless from a physical point of view but takes boring to a brand new level. Some friends stopped by and had lunch with us; we spent some time talking and that helped the day go by. I felt my brain getting fuzzier and more addled as the day goes on. I don't like the feeling and I have absolutely no control over what is going on. It's finally over and we go home, I'm very tired and fuzzy but, basically ok.*
>
> ***Day 2*** *Great day, part of what they infused me with was a steroid of some form to help clear the cobwebs and give me some strength; it works. We go*

the clinic in the afternoon to get the booster shot of Neulasta, which is to stimulate the bone marrow into the production of white blood cells, platelets and whatever other good things it makes. Thanks for warning me that it would feel like someone was shoving a hot coat hanger into my arm.

<u>Day 3</u> *All in all, not that bad of a day, feel a little flu-ish, actually a lot flu-ish, so I mainly stayed around the bed and napped.*

<u>Day 4</u> *Same as 3, achy, cramps, weak, no energy a baby could kick my tail. Appetite and everything else is ok, I am drinking lots of water (no beer).*

<u>Day 5</u> *I went to work. The "crappy feeling" is pretty much gone but my brain is still fuzzy, still weak, and no energy but I feel mostly human. I hit exhaustion around 2:30 (very tired), so I went home to bed and turned the phone off.*

Day 6 *I went to work, still feeling weak and fuzzy, but less fuzzy I think. I am running at ½ speed, 50% burner or what ever one might use to describe it – just not up to speed. My big bones, including my femur, damaged knees, collar bones, scapula and sternum all started aching. I was warned that this might happen as it is evidence that the Neulasta has gotten the bones working. Well, I guess that this isn't so bad.*

Day 7 *Yes, it is that bad. My bones hurt a lot, almost crippling, I can barely walk. In general, there is no position – sitting, lying down, standing, nothing that feels decent. Hello Hydrocordone!*

Day 8 *Ok, we can live with this if this is all there is to it. I feel fortunate because there has been minimal throwing up, minimal loss of appetite or anything to really complain about other than the bone thing and being so incredibly tired. I haven't missed any work yet and have been able to be fairly sociable. I still don't sleep well, but with all the new stuff going on in my body I guess I can understand it. The sleep aid the doctor gave me just doesn't get the job done because the brain just won't shut down. It is running constantly and will not shut down long enough to allow sleep. I can't describe how tired I feel.*

Each infusion over the ensuing months went pretty much the same way. There was however, a buildup effect and the more chemo I took, the greater the residual effect became. Increasingly, I fell victim to more and more of the side effects.

It is February 3, 2009 and I am getting the last infusion of the "big ones" (four hour infusion of Adriamycin /Cytoxin). From here on out, the infusions will be Taxotere, which will take much less time "on the bag". Taxotere is designed to attack the cancer cells while they are in a different stage of development than either of the two previous drugs did, thus completing the killing cycle.

This will be four cycles with three weeks between. I guess this stuff is a bad boy because even using the Nuelasta booster, it takes three weeks to recover. I can't wait to get started. Actually, I can't wait to get done. I have not been able to work a full day so I am now at home full-time and spending my time healing.

I guess I have been lucky with the A/C because I haven't had all the side affects that I could have had and they haven't been as severe as they were expected to be. I was told that all my hair would probably be gone by the start of the second infusion and I still have what I started with, which wasn't much anyway.

They guarantee that the Taxotere will finish what the A/C started. We will see, now it's a challenge to keep it, of course I have no control of the event but it is a new game for me to play.

I have a 24/7 cold-like congestion. It has been going on since the beginning. I was told that most people have a runny nose for the duration of treatment. I guess I am lucky because it runs in and collects in my throat rather than out collecting on my beard. That's lucky ? I guess.

This event has visibly aged my skin, probably the rest of my body too. My skin looks like elephant/chicken skin now and practically bleeds when you look at it for too long. That's a bit freaky because it seems like I have aged years instead of months and it has only been a matter of weeks.

My fingers don't work very well and playing my 12 string guitar now sounds like a beginner instead of someone who has been playing for 50 years. The fingers aren't as fast they used to be and are nowhere near accurate enough to make the chords sound right (they just don't hit in the right spot). However, I can still play bass as it is only one string at a time.

The chemo reaction is like a bell curve. At first it was a slow, shallow creep to the bottom (not too deep maybe an inch below the line of break-down-discomfort) then a rapid recovery back to where you started. Now, it is a rapid descent to a deeper (10 inches), wider trench of feeling truly rotten – spending much more time at the bottom and taking longer to get back up to a place that is now below where you started.

I still get pretty tired around 3:00 in the afternoon and usually need a nap. I have lost about 15 pounds, which is not such a bad thing. Most foods taste ok, I just fill up faster for some reason; I guess I'm too tired to eat.

There are eleven weeks, three days and six hours left until I should be done with chemo.

Somewhere during its use, the port site had become infected and the skin covering the port was beginning to degrade. The skin turned into an open sore then a blister and you could actually see the port.

If this was not brought under control, it might be necessary to stop my chemo treatment and put in another port. I did not want more surgery and an interruption to the chemo schedule was not a good thing.

Neither of these options were good choices. Dr. E decided to try to salvage the port by covering the open skin area with "Dermabond" (contact cement for the skin). It worked – the skin healed and we were able to continue with treatment. I thought that idea was thinking outside the box. Ironically, cementing things was a solution I could have thought of from my line of work.

Taxotere Infusions

I had my second Taxotere infusion Tuesday, March 17 and as usual, as a precursor to the infusion, I have my blood drawn and see my Doctor. I have had a complete physical (except for the bend over) every three weeks since December 8 – they are keeping good track of me. My blood work is over the top in excellence with high white blood count and strong Hemoglobin count.

My Oncologist is delighted with my progress and reaction to the drugs. My blood pressure maintains a steady 120/78 with a 65 to 70 pulse. He called me a chemo-taking machine as I have had minimal reaction to the really bad, normal occurrences. If my problems with chemo can be described as minimal, I can only imagine what others experience.

By now, he had expected that most of my body hair would be gone and that I would have had mouth sores, continual diarrhea, loss of some fingernails, and neuropathy in my fingers and toes. I have experienced minimal symptoms of the above and although it is not over yet, the end of chemo is very near (April 28). He said that I have an extremely strong system that is fighting back as hard as the chemo is so he sees no reason to expect less that a perfect final outcome.

I had initially told him that I was looking for at least 15 more years of life so I could get into my mid 70s, he feels now that this is short sighted. My body is providing an ideal battle- ground for the chemo to do its work. I personally believe that my ability to fight is based on my diet, because we all have heard that you are what you eat so if you need to be a chemo-taking machine you need to eat in the following manner:

Breakfast consists of eggs, sausage or bacon, juice, milk, cheerios, a banana, waffle or pancake or what ever combination you choose and a cup of coffee to get the bowels started. Lunch is whatever is available wherever you end up at that time. Supper is chicken, Tilapia, salmon, steak, ribs, some green stuff, bread, Miller Light or Robert Mondavi Select Reserve Merlot followed by a Metamucil chaser. On occasion, it doesn't hurt to throw in a prime rib, lobster or scallops. Ok enough of that.

I have had consultation with a Radiation Oncologist regarding the final stage of my cancer treatment, Radiation Therapy. I have teetered on the fence regarding radiation because there is such a good possibility that it can contribute to the onset of Lymphedema in my left (dominant) arm, possibly rendering it less than useful.

If this happens, I start missing out on a lot of my life that I enjoy (playing instruments, hugging grandchildren, wife, children and support babes) so

I have been reluctant to consider it until now. With as much as they know about this disease, the doctors admit that there is much that they don't know.

With this knowledge, caution and the implementation of all treatments that they do know to work, is advised. Since day one, every single doctor has recommended doing everything possible because you do not get a second chance to attack this disease the first time.

If something gets missed, on the first go around, you spend the rest of your life chasing it around your body, only finding it when it has caused cancer somewhere else. This is not an interesting idea to me. The final "push me off the fence" came from the radiation oncologist who gave me the "makes sense" that I needed.

I don't require total understanding of the subject but it needs to make sense to me before I will do it; here goes.

I have been under the understanding that the surgeon removed all of the cancer and the chemo was on a search-and-destroy mission to get rid of microscopic cells that may have escaped the surgery and taken up residence elsewhere. That basic premise is ok but not complete. I wondered why they recommended that I endure radiation to kill cancer cells that have either been removed or are being chased down by chemo.

This doesn't make any sense, so I was thinking, "I'm not doing this". The new information is that an area the size of a head of a pin can first of all, not be detected by any means available and secondly, can contain 10s of thousands of cancer cells just looking for a place to go. These cells if any, will be found in and around the surgery site. The new information also is that chemo does not always work effectively around scar tissue; radiation does. Now this becomes a no brainer, on to radiation for 5 weeks.

I have re-visited the BRCA topic with my oncologist for the purpose of gaining information for my daughters, to assist them in making decisions with which they may be faced. The overwhelming response from him and others is that there is still a ton of unknowns out there regarding genetics and with my situation being unique, they may never be able to find what actually set me off.

Equally puzzling is why am I so well equipped to fight cancer. My insurance will pay for further genetic testing only if it is being done to make decisions regarding further surgery on me – not for research of either of the other reasons (why I got it or why I fight so well).

Well obviously, there is no further surgery necessary on me at this time and no diagnostic information can be gained for such surgery, so why bother to test. The individual genetics are so diverse, there may be genetics from my daughters' mother that cancel or over ride mine or add a new dimension so, they really need to do individual tests or get into some study to be sure. And what would they do with the information? Increase their vigilance? They need to do that anyway.

Understanding Radiation Treatment

Preparing for radiation treatment, I find I was still having some serious debates raging regarding the need for Radiation therapy after the chemo is done. I need some education here to decide if I want it or not. A Radiation Oncologist obviously would say that it was absolutely necessary to complete the treatment.

My chemo oncologist indicated initially to me that I did not have to do the chemo treatment because the surgery supposedly removed all the cancer. If I skipped it, there was a 17% chance that I would live the rest of my life cancer free. If I took the chemo, there was an 83% chance that I would live cancer free – a "no brainer" there. However, I need the same type of percentage information regarding radiation. All whom I had talked to and everything that I had read agreed that radiation therapy will probably harden up and change the skin that was radiated. Most importantly, this can trigger the onset of Lymphedema, which was my most upsetting concern at the time.

I still have that "last time I saw my mother alive" picture in my mind (left arm wrapped and in a sling). Lymphedema therapy may require wrapping and sometimes slinging the affected arm. My mother had cancer in her left breast and had major surgery to her left side. I know intellectually, that her surgery was barbaric in comparison to mine.

Treatments are so much better now than they were then due to the advances made and things learned from all the women who have gone before me. However, since I am evidently following in her footsteps, I needed more info. After much discussion with the Radiation Oncologist, the decision was finally made to go through with the radiation therapy. The final fact presented to me was the issue that chemo does not work at its best in scar tissue. It apparently works well in good tissue but not well in scar tissue. Scar tissue was in the area of the surgery and the surgery was where the cancer was, so the decision then became logical.

An area the size of the head of a pin could contain thousands of cancer cells. Wouldn't it be a shame to go through all that I have already endured and miss one cell? One of the things that needed to be done prior to further treatment was to undergo another surgery to remove the port. That was good news, so off to Dr. E to finally get this thing out! To make an understatement, I had grown to hate the port.

Even though it was necessary to make me better, it was a constant reminder that I had cancer and was under treatment for such an ugly disease. It was uncomfortable and I still had the idea in my head that it could come apart and I would bleed out in my sleep. Like I said earlier, my mind can be my own worst enemy.

The Radiation Center

The people at the radiation clinic were extremely supportive. The equipment is extremely sophisticated and the operation of it is consequently really high-tech.

My first visit in there was spent getting positioned for treatment. It was imperative that I be in exactly the same position for each treatment, so an outline was made of me lying on my back in the proper treatment position. I will not get all technical here because I do not have the knowledge to do so, but I will relate the experience.

The machine was huge. It was what they call a linear accelerator and it is designed to deliver a specific dosage of radiation to a specific place on my body exactly the same every time. I was positioned on my back with my arms extended over my head and my head turned to the right. The mold that was made of me in this position was set on the table.

By laying down on it, I was placed on the table in exactly the same position each time. Additionally, three "freckles" were tattooed onto my chest so that once I was in position on the table, the table could be moved as necessary to line up exactly to those marks, using guide lasers. These lasers were part of the swing arm on the machine that delivered the dosage of radiation.

I was the first male bi-lateral mastectomy for many of the people in the center so I got more than my share of attention; I never felt uncomfortable, I just wanted to get the whole thing over with. The people were great; they had a great sense of humor and enough professionalism to know when and when not to use it.

Each "session" took about fifteen minutes, most of which was used getting me in the proper position for treatment. With each successive treatment, I got better at getting into position so eventually, the total time lessened.

Each treatment involved three passes by the machine. One was a glancing shot from right to left above my chest, next was a glancing shot from bottom to top under my left axilla and the third moved straight on between my shoulder and neck on the left side. Each was calculated to treat a specific area of skin for a measured length of time (seconds) and to deliver a specific dosage of radiation.

I felt nothing during the procedure and as I said earlier, once I was in position it only took a few minutes to receive the treatment. The schedule was for me to receive a treatment every day for five weeks in a row. Wow, a lot of driving and preparing for such a short procedure.

The first of several treatments had little effect on me as far as I could tell. However, as they continued past the half way point, they started taking their toll. The treated area started to get red and tender. It felt like a sunburn was going on and of course, I had not been out in the sun. I was also getting increasingly tired with each treatment.

There was a build-up affect much like that with the chemo and I was really beginning to drag. Blood was drawn after every fifth session to make sure that minimal damage was occurring to my blood during the process.

When the treatment was complete, I was sent on my way with a congratulatory balloon signed by all the people who had worked on me. My left chest was the color of a tomato with the texture of an old shoe.

The chest hair in the treated area was completely burned off and on my back, left shoulder, was a reflective burn from the table.

New Found Emotion: Physically speaking, I had a flat area to work with, so I imagine that the treatment I underwent was more simple than that of a woman who had a breast to save and to work around.

Also, my chest had been exposed to the sun and elements for a lot of my life, as I worked outside in the summers, so I would expect for the skin to be tougher than that of a woman. I really did not care about the final appearance of all the treatment.

I already had an 18 inch scar across my chest, so what if the hair is burned off and the skin is a little tough. My "beach-dude" days were over so it did not really matter to me. What about a woman though, it certainly would matter to her.

I completed the treatments and was told that all of this was normal and that I was finally free of cancer. It was a new feeling to look forward and realize that I was done – cancer free.

Let's Add Some Insult To Injury

During the initial work-up to identify where all of my breast cancer was located, a screening process called a PET scan was used. I was injected with a dye that was designed to seek out areas of high metabolic activity (cancer cells) and fluoresced them on CT image.

This gave the surgeon a "roadmap" to follow of where to cut to get the cancer out. I was informed that on the end of the report was an "oh, by the way" note, that stated that metabolic activity was identified on the left prostate. I had not paid much attention to that information but kept it in the back of my mind.

During one of the scheduled blood tests during radiation, I asked if they could get a PSA reading. My chemo oncologist said that such a reading during chemo would be extremely irregular and not worth the trouble to do until my system had a chance to settle down from all the chemotherapy drugs. The results taken later, during radiation treatment, came back at a 3.8, which was very high for me; I was usually under 1.0. This news sent me off to a urologist for a biopsy.

A prostate biopsy is one of the most uncomfortable things I have ever gone through. A device about the diameter of a golf club handle is inserted through the rectum and positioned on top of the prostate. I am not sure exactly how it works but, it was much like the biopsy for the breast cancer where you hear the staple gun "snap".

With this, a needle shoots through your colon into the gland and retrieves a sampling of what is there. My urologist took twelve samples (like a clock face) so he could get a complete, all around picture of the prostate. This was not extremely painful, but it was highly uncomfortable.

You are able to get yourself home ok and may have some spotty bleeding that doesn't last long. The results came back and 50% of the samples, all on the left side by the way, were positive for cancer. The saving grace here is that it was caught at a very early stage, it was not very active and was contained within the prostate.

Robotic-Assisted Laparoscopic Radical Prostatectomy

Surgery, Friday

The following is a diary of the prostatetectomy "experience".

Friday we checked into the hospital early because I was number one on the taxiway to take off. "Early" meant that I had to arrive at 5:15 AM for a procedure that would not start until 7:30, at the earliest. We live two counties away from the hospital so that means out of bed at 4:15. It really did not matter to me because I would be asleep for most of the day, but it was destined to be rough on my wife. I arrived at the hospital and was hooked up to the familiar equipment. I spoke to the Doctor and wished him a really, really, really good day – I kissed Sandy and that's about all I remember.

I understand that in the procedure room, you are positioned on your back with your feet in stirrups (to spread the pelvic area) with your entire body tilted slightly head down, (so gravity could move intestines etc. away from the actual surgery area). I am also convinced that they put a cement block under the small of your back to make sure that your back hurts when you wake up. It worked.

The surgeon reported to my wife that my procedure went fine. Evidently, there was some difficulty navigating through some old scar tissue from a previous laparoscopic surgery, and I think that he also ran into some mesh from a previous hernia repair. He had intended to leave the catheter in for one week initially but because of the snags, extended to two weeks.

Waking up after this surgery is just like waking up after any surgery, not fun. You are full of gas, disoriented, aching, mouth is dry, need to use the restroom, want to throw up. Actually, I am fortunate in the throw-up area because I tolerate the anesthesia pretty well. The hospital bed is still one of the most uncomfortable things ever invented. The good ones allow you to adjust the head, foot or knees up or down, or to make it flat. With this, you can distribute the pain to other parts of your body that were not directly affected by the surgery.

I was in the hospital bed around 1 pm. On my back, hooked up to oxygen, and had the IV still in my arm. I use the right arm for IV and blood pressure since I am considered to be a lymphedema risk because of all the surgery that was done in my left axilla. The doctors have told me to minimize the possibility of trauma to the left arm so I do. I had a pretty good load of morphine on board so I did not feel too badly. I had a light meal for dinner and my wife went home to relax and get some sleep.

Day One, Saturday

I woke up the next day to the oxygen sensor alarm going off because I was not breathing deep enough to satisfy the machine that monitors how much oxygen is in my blood. Well EXCUSE ME, I was sleeping! My right forearm looked like I was a long time drug user because it seemed that everyone in the hospital who had a needle, came in and took a blood sample from me. I still had some morphine in me, which gave me a false sense of how I really felt. I had some breakfast, got up and walked and started to feel pretty happy with how tough I must be because it's not THAT bad. Sandy got there, the Doctor came in, we talked and he discharged me and off we went.

By the time we got home, the drugs were wearing off and I found out that I'm not such a tough guy after all. It felt as if somehow when I was asleep, someone slipped some razor blades into me and the intestinal gas was moving those blades around inside my colon. I cannot describe how painful that gas moving around was. Additionally, my body was bloated from the gas that had been injected into me for the procedure and the tissue that had been cut, sutured or moved around was swollen. Everything hurt and there was no more available morphine. To my luck, I had some 750 mg Vicodin, which gave some relief.

Day Two, Sunday

Sunday, what a glorious day. I woke up got out of bed, drained my urine bag and POOPED. Glorious poop. Finally some of the intestinal gas was moving out rather than around and what a difference that made! At least one system was getting back on the grid. I was still pretty bloated from the surgery gas, and was still swollen, but I was generally improving.

The incision areas still hurt quite a bit and getting up, down or anywhere hurts when the abdomen is all cut up. It seems that we become amazingly aware of how much we use our abdomen muscles when there is an incision to work around. I should have thought of this before but a walker (for support by the arms) would have been really useful for getting in and out of chairs, the bed, on and off the toilet etc. I will have to remember that for next time.

By now, I was pretty much weaned off of Sandy changing and emptying my urine bags and was fairly self-sufficient. I was able to move around with improved ease, which helped me perform more normal tasks. I was not back to normal eating habits yet but was moving food from one end to the other – this is a step in the right direction. Sleep was acceptable with the help of the Vicodin, and at this point, I felt that I could start healing and dealing with the joy of the catheter.

Day Three, Monday

Now that the pain was pretty much under control, systems were coming back on line and I was eating and sleeping pretty well, I had developed some spare time to ponder the catheter. I knew that it was there because you can't miss it but, it hadn't been pondered yet. The catheter is a rubber tube, very soft to the touch and the diameter of a rolling pin. Not really, Sandy said that it is "20 French", which actually translates to me as the diameter of a pencil. It has a saline-filled bulb at the top, which holds it in my bladder, located where the urethra was sewn back to it. The bulb holds the top of the catheter in place.

The bottom is anchored to my thigh where the bags get attached. Here comes the epiphany, as I move around, since both ends of the catheter are fixed, my body moves up and down the catheter, not with it. This is where the instructions regarding keeping the catheter clean come into play. Obviously, anything stuck to the catheter would move in and out with the catheter as I move. It is a really good idea to keep it clean and lubricated!

Day Four, Tuesday

Everything is improving. Pain is lessening, mobility is improving, bowel is moving but abdomen swelling not going down much, still pretty blown up. Still have pain from the "stab wounds" but in the big picture, it's not worth mentioning. No sit-ups today, or this month for that matter. No more pondering the catheter, I have accepted it as my friend now and I count the days until it can come out and I can move towards "back to normal". Eight days to go for catheter removal.

Days Five through Thirteen

Daily entries have stopped here because I don't feel all that badly. I still experience pain from the wounds but they are hurting less every day. The only real discomfort is the catheter but I can stand that (not that I really have a choice.)

Day Thirteen

The catheter came out on day number thirteen. This was not fun but it marks the beginning of the final phase of healing. The removal of the catheter was not as bad as I had expected. The nurse simply deflated the bulb on the end (in my bladder) and pulled it out. I had prepared myself for her pulling barb wire out and was pleasantly surprised. Now that the catheter is out, it becomes a matter of getting the urinary tract back on line.

I have been sleeping great at night because there has been no need to get up to relieve myself as it has been draining into the bag. Basically that entire system had been on auto pilot and I have had nothing to do but to maintain the bag. Now I have to be concerned with squirts and dribbles. Not that big a deal for now as I am sure that this too shall pass.

I have learned that the prostate acts as a passive constrictor type of valve on the urethra. With it gone, there is no restriction on the urethra to retain urine once it is beyond the muscle in the bladder. Now when I shift unexpectedly (stand up, sit down twist or the like) there is a potential for a little squirt of urine.

My doctor told me to do some Kagel exercises which tighten a muscle in your lower abdomen. By doing a "Kagel" prior to moving, I can avoid the dribbles; it very soon becomes second nature and does not present a problem.

> ***Guy Note:*** *This process of the prostate swelling up and restricting your urine flow is a gradual thing; over the years you are not aware of the decreased flow. Now that it has been removed, the flow is incredible, you can empty 10 gallons of urine in less than 10 seconds, extreme power, 20 foot arc if you are outside. What a difference. I am glad that it is gone, my psa now is 0.02 or undetectable.*

The Bucket List

Below is my current "Bucket List". Like it or not, this whole realization of my mortality has triggered the development of such a list. It is a good thing and should be taken exactly as such because it identifies things to look forward to doing. It is open to additions at any time but not open to taking away from.

- ✓ *Cruise to Hawaii, October 2009 (done)*
- ✓ *Shuttle launch at Helene's (done)*
- ✓ *Visit Cathy in Denver (Koman thing Oct 3, 2009) (done)*
- ✓ *One more run to Alaska (cruise portion only) with our long time friends Art and Cheryl May 2010 (done)*
- ✓ *Eat lunch at Fisherman's Wharf (remembrance of "crab for dad day")*
- ✓ *Napa/Sonoma Valley wine tour*
- ✓ *Great Lakes / Canada tour in fall*
- ✓ *Sandy play in the snow in upstate New York*
- ✓ *Raise at least one of my grandsons as a Master Mason in the lodge that I was Master of in 2008 (this would be incredible because it is so rare an event)*
- ✓ *Attend all of our grandchildren's weddings*
- ✓ *Meet at least one great grand baby.*

The Celebration

My sister, who is a twenty-one year breast cancer survivor, lives out in Colorado and has become quite involved with the Susan G. Komen organization in that area. There was a "Race for the Cure" in early October and she invited my wife and me out there to participate in my first "race" as a survivor.

Her daughter would also participate with us in her first walk as a survivor, as well as our stepmother, who is an eighteen-year survivor. We made our plane reservations and off we went to Colorado.

As we moved up the escalator into the baggage reception area, I was incredibly surprised to find most of my family waiting. Meeting us at the airport were all of my children, some grandchildren, my stepmother, sister and her husband, niece, brother, cousin and her husband, my sister's family, in-laws and children and some friends of both families – all in pink and blue t-shirts.

My wife knew what was going on but I did not have a clue. It was a tremendous surprise and turned out to be a fantastic weekend. Cathy had done a great amount of planning to enable the nearly flawless pulling off of the event. Sleeping and transportation arrangements were all set up as well as a great train adventure on Saturday.

One of my daughters had written and recorded a song of my cancer journey that was played on the PA system at the event; it was very moving. All in all a very well thought out and loving treat. Perhaps going to Colorado in October will become a tradition. The lyrics to the song that was played at the event follow on the next page. The song summarizes the story of breast cancer in my family, as it walks through my childhood, to now.

The "little boys" represent myself and my brother Ralph, and the "little girl" is my sister Cathy. The "mama" is of course, my own mother who died of breast cancer when I was young. "The girls" are my three daughters, Kellie, Lorin and Aj.

Note from Lorin – *"One day, we were all sitting around talking about the cancer that runs in the family, Dad commented that if he could go through it himself, and prevent his three girls from going through what his mother did…that he would. That is the thought that inspired the song, and as "music" is a family gift passed down to all from his mother, we expressed the multiple gifts that came through in these lyrics. This song hit me all at once and I cried the entire time while I scribbled it down as fast as I could. I still have that "yellow pad" sheet of paper and it's crinkled from being wet! The lyrics follow on the next page and I have arranged for ALL proceeds of "The Gift of Love" to go to cancer research."*

The Gift Of Love

Song Written for Dad…By Lorin Harmon Sourbeck

Little boys need their mama…And a little girl does too
She played her songs and sang for them as mothers often do
She said "the gift of love is in this song, as I sing it now to you
Sleep tight, my babies, I'll be watching over you.

The kids, they get older their mama wasn't doing well
Doctors, they did all they could but as her eyelids slowly fell…
She said "the gift of love is in this song, and I pass it on to you
I'll sleep tight, my babies, I'll be watching over you.

You know it's hard, but you just grow up the boy made a family
He heard the song in their voices his mother's love was in all three
He said "the gift of love is in this song, as I sing it now to you.
My mama gave me love in music. It is a gift…you have it too.

The man sat down and prayed one night… God and momma,- please hear me
If someone has to get that cancer – not my girls, give it to me…
He heard "the gift of love is in the song, I see that love got into you
Your wish, it will be granted so let my strength carry you.

Well he finished up his chemo and the radiation too
And his girls came together, Dad ,we have a song for you
Your gift of love is in our song, as we sing it now to you
God took your gift of love and He gave it back to you

Your gift of love is in our song, can you hear your momma too
God took your gift of life and He gave it back to you

Visit www.SongsForCause.org for a recording.

The Gift Of Love

By Lorin Harmon Sourbeck

My Dad… cancer, wow. As my favorite memories poured through, I recalled days as a kid, when the live music that played in our living room on weekends. I remember my dad teaching us how to play guitar and taking me out to play bluegrass with him.

And I remember my birthday one year when my birthday card said that the present was in the bathtub. As I slid open the glass door of the tub, I saw the worn out, beat up black case of my dad's first-born guitar. "The Gibson"… that his mom gave to him when he was a teenager, before she died. I cried then, and do again as I write this. I used that guitar in recording the song I wrote for my Dad. As I inserted on a previous page, the song, "The Gift of Love" hit me all at once. I wrote it as fast as I could with tears running down my face, soaking the yellow pad of paper. I still have it – it lives with the first recording of the song.

Thanks to the courtesy of the people at the Komen event above in Colorado that year, they played the song over the big stage speakers. I handed dad the CD, which includes cover & story. He's holding it in the photo above. He cried for a long time. Dad has never showed emotion… but sometimes we'll catch an escaping smirk or if we're lucky, a red-cheeked laugh. When we do get a reaction out of him, we know "we got him"… so in this case… I know the message was delivered. ☺ I love you Dad . (Below) Frank Hearing The Song For The First Time

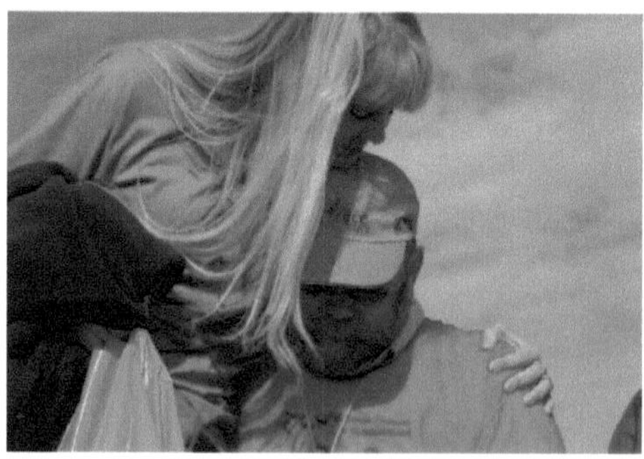

The song is available for download on www.songsforcause.org. ALL proceeds go to breast cancer research in hope for a healthy future for all families dealing with this.

So Now What

Surviving two primary cancers in one year is not un-heard of I guess but it is something that certainly should go down in some record book. I feel as though I should win a prize like a new car or something for doing such a thing, but the prize really is to be able to write this. It has been a miserable year; it has been scary, painful and expensive. It has however been a good year because much has been learned and lived.

I have grown much closer to my family. I have a bond with my sister, my stepmother and my niece that is strong and loving but not easy to talk about because of the subject matter. I have a bond with millions of women whom I do not even know. I have a closer bond with my mother as she also had breast cancer; fortunately, some of us have survived. I love my wife more because she has spent so much of herself in helping me this year, I can only hope that it has not taken too much from her strength. I also realized that, although I would, I hope that I never have to do the same for her.

I have grown closer to my children. We all found out in 2009 that "Dad" is not bullet proof. Hopefully, they have realized that life is very short and there really is no time for nonsense. Hopefully, they have learned that tomorrow they could wake up and find that I might not be there.

I recall when my mother died but more strikingly when my father died, that the next morning, I woke up and realized that for the first time in my life, my daddy wasn't there. It was a lonely, unprotected feeling but we all must go through it eventually. I hope that my children have learned that tomorrow one of them may not be with us and that the last thing said or done may have to last forever. Make it a good thing.

I have also decided that "tomorrow" is more important that the "stuff" we have accumulated. "Stuff" is nice and in many ways is a measure of your success, but "stuff" will not keep you breathing and will do you no good after you are gone. Tomorrow needs to be happy and fun and there is just no substitution for it. Make it that way.

I am a monster believer in early detection. As a male, I was not looking for breast cancer in myself. We are flooded by the media regarding monthly checks for women, breast cancer awareness, mammograms, walks, races and on and on. This is a good thing and it needs to be kept up and maybe even stepped-up. However, I would like to see at least some inkling of recognition or warning for men. It does not have to be on the same scale as women's awareness but how about just an honorable mention to at least give men a fair warning.

In early December of 2008, about a month after the mastectomy surgery, an anchorwoman from a local CBS TV station did a video interview with me at Dr. E's office. The interview was aired later that evening. Heather Van Nest of WTSP "10 Connects News" maintains a vigilant stand on womens' breast cancer issues by doing monthly reminders to "check yourself" on the 10th of each month. She is a great believer of early detection and has probably saved lives with her awareness.

She took an interest in my case because it was breast cancer related and I am sure that someone somewhere benefited from seeing her piece. That video can be viewed on the "Real Men Get Breast Cancer" website.

Had I been on alert for breast cancer, I might have avoided the extent of treatment I had to go through. I might have detected my lump at an earlier stage of development, before it had spread and might have avoided the extent of surgery the chemotherapy and the radiation.

Perhaps my lump was detected as early as it could have been and my course of treatment was destined. I will never know. The prostate cancer was detected in its earliest stages. Consequently, treatment necessary although radical, was minimal and curative.

This last year can be described as an all-out assault on my body. I have been attacked by surgeries, chemotherapy and radiation. Along the way I have been cut, sewn, radiated, anesthetized, drained, poked, listened to, scanned, pressurized, depressurized and "sampled". So now what is left of the experiment?

All of the hair that I lost during chemo has come back, in some cases thicker and darker. I have no visible remaining effects of the chemo treatment. The area of my chest that was radiated has softened up, gotten less red and the hair is growing back where it was burned off.

My right arm bears no effects of the axilla surgery other than a ten-inch scar and a touch of numbness in the scar area. The left arm however, my primary use arm is a different story.

I have the same ten inch scar as on the right side, but the left side scar did not heal as well. It had an infection during the draining stage of healing and re-attached itself to my chest cavity in two stages rather than one. The result is a ridge affect where it should be smooth.

The left axilla had quite a bit of surgery done and as a result, there is far more scar tissue to deal with. My left triceps is numb from my shoulder to my elbow and I have a constant feeling of "banging your funny bone" that really never goes away. The axilla itself also is numb. My range of motion is limited because of the scar tissue and if I push it by stretching too far, it pays me back with a big shot of ouch. I have lost a lot of strength in my left arm and a lot of mobility. I can no longer use the construction tools that I have used my entire life; I can't climb a ladder or throw a ball. However, I do have my life though and that is reward enough.

A lot of prayers were said this year by a lot of people and I appreciate each and every one of them. Sometimes I wonder, who are we to interfere with the Lord's work? He gave me the cancer but He also provided a method of getting rid of it so I guess that is what He wants me to do.

I will keep fighting this disease as long as I can and as long as I need to. I have asked, "why me". Why did I have to go through all this. The only answer that works is that I was going to get my cancers any way, I was fortunate enough to get them while I was strong enough and healthy enough to beat them. I wish the same for you.

Final Guy Note: *Throughout this writing I have used the "Guy notes" as an opportunity to step out of the patient role, let my sense of humor loose and just be a male. It's good being a guy because we get away with a lot of stuff due to the fact that nobody expects us to have any emotions or to have a sensitive side.*

We are expected to hang out, drink beer, watch NASCAR, football, barbeque, scratch, belch, pick, fish, etc., etc. But surprise, we are all not that way; I now excuse myself after a belch (if there is someone around). This humbling experience has made me look at some things differently and has allowed me to realize that I am not bulletproof and that it is ok to spontaneously hug someone even if that someone is a guy. A hug is a sign of "I like you, I thank you, I appreciate you, I am glad to see you" and so much more. Peace.

2009 Guess What

Well, the year from hell is finally over but it has not been without its good points.

On December 21, I had blood drawn at my oncologist office and met with him yesterday December 30 to discuss the results of the test. As a cancer survivor, there are now certain proteins in my blood (as are in Helene's, Cathy's and Ashlie's) that can be identified as part of a Complete Metabolic Panel (CMP).

These proteins are at a very specific level provided there is no breast cancer in my system; if the levels are higher than specified, there is cancer. My levels indicate that I am totally cancer free. In addition, my PSA is 0.02 and the prostate node dissection came back all clear. I must maintain the Tamoxifen regimen for 4 ½ more years and see my Oncologist for blood tests twice a year to check the protein levels.

My Oncologist is basically my primary now, as he knows more about my body chemistry than anyone else. After he examined me yesterday, he stood back and grinned and told me that if he hadn't seen my surgery scars and hadn't received a report from my Urologist that I had had a radical prostectomy, he would not believe it. He said that I looked that good. He further stated that had he not been personally involved with my treatment last year, he would not believe all that I had been through.

He stated that my heart and lungs were in the general condition of someone half my age. I still maintain a 128/78 blood pressure, low 60's resting heart rate, and have no cholesterol problems. I am almost back to my four miles a day walk and "Dude" is happy.

My left axilla still hurts and restricts my left arm movement. I guess I will just have to live with it because it is unlikely to get much better. What all this proves is that with some good medical treatment, some good home caring, a lot of prayers from family and friends, some luck and especially with a lot of help from "The Big Guy", you can beat almost anything. Thanks for your love, prayers and support, 2010 is going to ROCK.

Where Do You Go From Here?

Ok, so you got cancer, sorry about that, it's rotten luck but somebody has to do it or there would be a lot of people suddenly out of work if a cure was found. You had your surgery, chemo and radiation and are now on a maintenance drug like Tamoxifen or something else to keep you "cancer free" for five years; after then, your risk of recurrence goes down, they say.

You never really get the thought of having cancer out of your mind because you have your blood drawn every six months and it is checked to find out if there is any significant change in your protein levels. That experience is good for your blood pressure because you get all wound up waiting for the results (once I was 190/140 with a pulse of 85). Got the results, found out that I was ok and the BP went down to its normal 130/76 with a 65 pulse. The entire experience of having cancer is a roller coaster ride that I guess you never really get off of.

Last year I found a couple of lumps that concerned me so I took them to Dr. Echevarria so he could check them out. It was determined that a lump in my neck was probably the re-emergence of a previously removed lypoma. A lump in my right axilla was undetermined by a PET scan so he ordered a MRI scan and then a CT scan. It was finally determined that whatever is was or is, was non cancerous scar tissue so we decided to leave it alone.

As annoying and expensive as these tests were to take, I came away from the experience knowing that they could find no cancer anywhere in my body. The more I thought about this discovery, the happier I became because I was convinced that at this time, there really was no cancer in me. The surgery worked; the chemo worked; the radiation worked and the Tamoxifen was working. For the first time since this nightmare started, I actually felt that I had won. I have won, I beat cancer; two of them. I am bad to the bone.

The thing is, we all are told that cancer usually comes back; not always, but probably. I realized that as bad as the entire experience was, it would have been much worse if I had not been in pretty good physical shape. I was strong and healthy and not suffering from any disease related physical limitations when I was diagnosed. Had it been otherwise, I probably would have experienced a fuller range of nastier reactions and would have felt much worse; therefore, I joined the local YMCA to regain my original strength and activity level so I will be strong should the cancer ever return. The YMCA has a program called "Livestrong" which is a 12 week physical conditioning program in association with Lance Armstrong and it is free to cancer survivors. Free is good, so I signed up.

I was assigned a trainer to assess my initial condition and was put through a battery of "tests" to determine how much torture I could probably endure throughout this training session. When I went to the first group session there were TWO of them assigned to my beatings not just the one who assessed me. For someone like me who has always felt like he was pretty much "a tough guy", it was unsettling to be under the direction of two women who could probably kick my butt. And that's another thing, why do all of these gyms show happy, young, physically fit people who can probably run to California and back and bench press a pickup truck when the reality is that the people going to the gyms look like me. Am I supposed to think that after some training and workouts I will look like them? Here's your sign. I should be the poster boy because looking like me is reality; none of us cancer survivors will ever look like them and be twenty years younger again. Oh well.

But it's all good. I joined the group class led by Marianne and Shandra which met on Monday for a ½ hour. I opted for a ½ hour personal training session on another day with Shandra rather than another ½ hour group session. It worked out well for me because the group was pretty generic so the exercises were in some cases, not very challenging for me. I could see the difficulty in tailoring an exercise program for such a diverse group of people but they did a great job by having me do the exercises faster or with a stronger band or whatever. The really good thing about the program is that you find yourself with other cancer survivors who have been through what you have been through and you are all on the same page. You all have the same get healthier and stronger attitude and all know what it is like to fear for your life and to be in such great pain and discomfort. The class lasted for 12 weeks and at the end I was "out processed" by repeating the original assessment tests to see if there was any improvement in my conditioning. There was a lot of improvement and I had lost some weight and made some new friends so the entire experience was a win, win, win. Marianne and Shandra are both very knowledgeable, compassionate and caring people; true assets to the YMCA.

Shandra worked me. She fed the exercises to me slowly, with weights lighter than I wanted to use but, she knew that too much would blow or pull something and that I would go backwards rather than forward if I pulled a muscle. She taught me a total body workout routine that I can do myself and I increase the weights as I feel necessary.

I have graduated "Livestrong" and I am on my own now responsible for my own training. I have been well taught so I will be fine but…I will miss my new friends and trainers.

I feel that some form of physical re-training or re-strengthening should be part of the cancer treatment routine so look for a "Livestrong Program" at your local YMCA or some form of directed exercise and just do it.

A note from Shandra

The fact that you picked up a book called "Real Men Get Breast Cancer" tells me that you or someone you love is dealing with the dreaded C word. I can tell you that before becoming a part of the LiveStrong at the Y program, I thought that cancer wasn't something that anyone wanted to talk about.

Now I know that everyone needs to talk about it, ask questions, and be proactive about their own health. So thank you Frank for having the courage to write this book, for taking charge of your health so that you are here to write this book, and not only for asking me to contribute to this new addition, but for educating me on the many aspects of living as a cancer survivor, that I did not know or understand.

You have made me both a better trainer and a better person.

So yes, I was the person that got to beat Frank up weekly and it was a pleasure! A little about me – I am married and the mother of 4 children ranging in age from 17 to 3 years old. I am a NASM certified Personal Trainer, a LiveStrong certified Trainer, and also a NASM certified Sports Nutrition Specialist. I run over 10 small group personal training classes a week at our local YMCA as well as train for LiveStrong, with both group LiveStrong classes and one-on-one clients.

To be clear, there is no "typical" LiveStrong participant. Everyone comes to us with different ability levels, different limitations, and different goals. I train all ages from a wonderful woman in her 30s to cranky old guys like Frank. Some come to me during Chemo, others post surgery, and some years after. That is what is great about our program, as long as you are a Cancer Survivor we welcome you and your family.

Exercise

The three things that all LiveStrong clients need, and generally all personal training clients need, are stretching, core and balance, and strength. What seems to be happening at our Y, is that most of the 50+ clients like our group classes.

Most come to us deconditioned, meaning they did not do much physical activity before their cancer occurred and most were told to take it easy post surgery. We work with them in a slower paced manner but always include hidden things that challenge their core and stability.

Balance seems to be the one thing most affected from chemo that makes getting back to a "new normal" the most challenging. Working on balance issues starts with the core. Simple ways to challenge your core is just standing on one foot or performing an exercise such as bicep curls while sitting on a stability ball. Walking a straight line while lifting and holding up each knee can be a challenge for many. But before you know it my clients are progressing to stepping up on a low step and doing a knee raise without a wobble!

Working with bands is also a great way to challenge the core and add strength moves.

My co-worker Marianne is a wonder with coming up with new ways to challenge our clients. What they don't realize is that the simple act of both putting on the band and removing the band is also our way of challenging their core and working on flexibility. Yes, we trainers can be super sneaky that way!

Strength moves, especially upper body, can be a challenge for many with mastectomies. Range of motion limitations from not just the mastectomy or reconstruction but more so from the removal of the lymph nodes tends to show up often. Other things we consider are lymphedema concerns. The one thing I can tell you is you need, **no you must,** use those upper body muscles, including chest, shoulders, and back. It's the old adage "use it or lose it".

Just simple 3 pound weights is what you can start with and simple moves like bicep curls on the ball, triceps kickbacks, overhead press are all great options. One of my favorite for the chest is a push up against the wall; the farther out you put your feet the more challenging it will be but you will be surprised at how quickly you will progress when you start using these muscles.

To address lymphedema issues, we try to stagger body parts when doing circuit training in our groups. That means we do one upper body move followed by a lower body move then return to the upper body. We also recommend that you make sure to use light weights and do not exercise to the point of exhaustion. If you were fitted for a compression sleeve we require you to wear that when you work out with us.

Stretching is something you need to do not just before and after exercise, but all day. At our YMCA we also offer a LiveStrong yoga class twice a week and Lisa is great at showing you how to safely do yoga and stretching. I encourage my clients to do things like "hang in the doorway" and "hold up the wall". "Hang in the doorway" is standing in the doorway with your arms spread and gently, very gently, pushing forward. Do not overextend, just feel that stretch through your chest. "Hold up the wall" is either sitting on the floor or standing with your back against the wall – shoulders too.

This makes you stand up straight instead of rolling your shoulders forward. This reminds me to check my posture as I am writing this too!

Exercising as part of a group makes getting out and moving so much more fun. The added benefit is you get to see that there are lots of other people dealing with the same issues as you and the friendships that I see form with each group are amazing. The people in your group know the names of the medications you are on and have either gone through what you are going through, or you get to help someone else face the same fears you did.

The group also helps keep you accountable, because you know when you miss a day the rest of the group will be sure to let you know they missed you the next time you come.

Nutrition

As part of the LiveStrong at the Y program we do not directly address nutrition, however if one of my clients ask me, I will be happy to talk to them about it privately.

Getting active is just one part of staying healthy. Your nutrition is just as important. Without the proper building blocks your body cannot repair itself and keep itself healthy. First you need to make sure you are staying hydrated. Purified water is the best thing for you. The universal rule of thumb is take your weight in pounds, divide it in half, and that is how many ounces of water you should drink each day. So, are you getting enough? Water will also help move all of those chemicals out of your system and keep your colon and bowels happy too.

The next thing I personally believe in is to keep your body alkaline. This helps with not just cell reconstruction and fat loss but studies have shown that cancer cells cannot form in an alkaline environment, but they love an acidic one! The best thing you can do is NOT drink coffee or sodas. Coffee is very acidic and sodas contain so much sugar… cancer cells just love sugar! Green products that contain Ionic alfalfa, spirulina and are sweetened with stevia, both taste good and are good for you!

Of course the other basics that you know, cut down on the processed and fast foods and eat more whole foods. An apple is better for you than apple sauce and apple juice is the worst choice of the three. I also encourage you to check out how much protein you take in each day and where it comes from. Lean proteins like chicken, fish, and turkey are preferable. Most women, especially, do not take in enough protein. I also firmly believe in eating smaller but more frequent meals. This helps to increase your metabolism, but more importantly you never get to that point where you are so hungry you eat anything, and everything, in sight!

Frank brought to my attention an interesting mindset that he deals with and that many other cancer survivors seem to also. In the back of their head they still see the image of that one patient they encountered during chemo that was extremely thin, fragile and weak. And they want to make sure that is never them. So whether they acknowledge it or not, having extra weight makes them feel strong and healthy. However, the extra weight can also lead to its own problems of high blood pressure, diabetes, stroke and mobility issues. So if you even think this may be you, I encourage you to talk to someone about it, because there is a difference between thin and sick and fit and healthy!

The most rewarding part of what I do is helping my clients discover they are so much stronger than they ever thought they were. The sense of accomplishment obtained in the gym bleeds out to all aspects of their lives. We provided a place for them to go to share both their triumphs and setbacks and make getting healthy a habit we hope will continue after our 12 weeks are up. So I highly encourage you to visit www.Livestrong.org and check out the Livestrong at the YMCA program nearest you. I would also be happy to answer any questions you may have, just look me up in the resources section of this book.

Here is the best compliment I have ever had. *"I love this girl! She made my life worth living again!"* G.R. LiveStrong Client

From left to right, Marianne, Frank & Shandra

Acknowledgements

It is obvious that I did not take this cancer journey alone, and that I certainly could not have survived it without help. I was fortunate in the fact that I was (and still am) in good overall health. I was suffering no consequences of the cancer so there were no other health issues to deal with and all attention and treatments were directed at the task of getting rid of the cancer.

People have said, "You have gone through so much" and "what an ordeal" and things like that. Although these statements are true, all I really brought to the fight was attitude and the battleground. I woke up every day and said "screw you cancer" or something to that effect and went to bed each night with the same attitude.

I dealt with the people who cared for me with a sense of humor and gratitude. I really did appreciate everything that they did to cure me and always try to find some humor in the things that we have to deal with.

We have to deal with them anyway so you may as well try to have some enjoyment. I want to thank the following for their part in my successful treatment.

Dr. David Echevarria, (Dr. E)
Dr. Anthony Brannan
Their staff at Tampa Surgical Associates

Dr. Christopher George &
His staff at Florida Cancer Specialists

Dr. Alison Calkins &
Her staff at Tampa Cancer Care Center

Dr. Frank Mastandrea &
His staff at Florida Urology Partners

St. Joseph's Hospital & Staff

My friends and family for prayers and support

Heather Van Nest for her never ending awareness
WTSP

My daughter Lorin for help in turning my ramblings into a book &writing for me the song, "Gift of Love", and choosing to donate all the proceeds to breast cancer research.

My wife Sandy for prayers, support, help, attitude and love

The Good Lord for all of the above and any loose ends.

In Dedication…

to those who have survived cancer...

to those who have not survived...

to the families of those who have fought cancer...

to those who have lived, loved and lost...

to those who research cancer to find a cure...

to those who want to support genetic research...

to those who want to support preventative health...

and to those who didn't get these answers in time.

www.ingramcontent.com/pod-product-compliance
Ingram Content Group UK Ltd.
Pitfield, Milton Keynes, MK11 3LW, UK
UKHW041923190726
13854UKWH00003B/1410